"The Lord Will Perfect That Which Concerns Me" (*and You!*)

Psalm 138:8 (Amplified)

By BARBARA ARBO

T

The Lord Will Perfect

Printed in the United States of America
ISBN: 979-8-9874866-6-5

Unless otherwise indicated, all Scripture quotations are taken from the Amplified Bible, Classic Edition as shown below.

Text Design: Lisa Simpson

To my husband, Steve:

a *good gift and a perfect, free, full gift from above . . .*

(James 1:17)

Preface

It is hard to believe it has been over 50 years since I prayed a simple prayer, unlocking the door of my heart to invite Christ's Lordship in.

This book, which recounts the early days of my walk with God, has circled the globe and turned out to be a blessing to so many people. We often have no idea how the victories we win through faith in God can help others, but they do!

It was time to update the original book, and in reading the story again, I realized it was best to present it as it was in the original transcript, with only minor edits.

Life has a way of complicating our understanding, but the simplicity of this story is for those who are just beginning their journey of faith in God and can be encouraged by these timeless truths.

I have been married for over 45 years now, have raised two sons, and have served the Lord in full-time ministry since 1981.

I will say that as I have "grown up" into a deeper relationship with God, I am more convinced than ever that to "see, say, and pray" God's Word are basic truths that continue to feed my faith and starve my doubts, as God continues to ". . . *perfect [those things that] concern me.*"

May the truths you read in the following pages convince you, too!

Barbara Arbo

Foreword

Words cannot express how delighted I am to have the opportunity to write the introduction to Barbara Arbo's book.

As I was thinking about what to say, a scripture came to me from Psalm 113:9, which speaks of God making a woman a joyful mother of spiritual children. Praise the Lord! Hallelujah! God has sent a "spiritual child" into my life named, Barb. She is like my very own daughter, and I love her with the kind of love only a spiritual mother has for a spiritual child that the Father has sent to her.

Barb came into my life when I was in New York ministering. I knew the moment I met her that she would be a special part of my life. It was instant love!

When she stopped to visit me in Fort Worth, Texas, on her way to Brazil (she thought that was where she was going) I was so glad she had come. One afternoon, we were on our way home from shopping, and I said, "Barb, I know you will be a very vital and important part of my life and ministry someday." Her tears began to flow, and she said, "Billie, I want to stay and be a part of your ministry. I will do anything — clean your house, cook for Dane and Kevin, be your secretary. . . Of course, I agreed because the Holy Spirit impressed me that very day that "someday" was now. She was a constant companion to me. She did all the things she said she would, plus more. She became my "spiritual daughter" just like Psalm 113:9 had promised.

She stayed with me for three years and I watched her become a mature woman of God, a wife (I performed the ceremony) and an ordained minister. She and her husband, Steve, were an active part of Vicki Jamison-Peterson Ministries before launching out into their own ministry. I watched her take the Word, put it forth in prayer, and I have seen the excellence of results. It is just like she says in her book — it produces!

I highly recommend this book. It will bless you as you read it by wonderfully uplifting your spirit. If you will use this as a guidebook in your prayer life, every circumstance, crisis, and problem will change as you begin to say what God's Word says about the situations in your life. It will change your prayer life!

By the way, if you were to ask me what Barb is really like, I would say she is a love-walking woman, as in 1 Corinthians 13:4-8. Thank you, Barb, for your vital part in my life, and thank you, Father, for this "spiritual child."

Billie Adams
Women of the Word — "WOW"
Now at Home with the Lord

Table of Contents

1

My Encounter With Reality — Jesus

Romans 8:3 became a reality to me in 1971. It says, "God has done what the Law could not do . . . Sending His own Son in the guise of sinful flesh [in the disguise of a sinful man, as if He was one] God... subdued, overcame, deprived [sin] of its power over all who accept that sacrifice."

On New Year's Eve in 1971, I accepted that sacrifice and Jesus became my Savior. I was twenty-one years old and had been on drugs since the tender age of fourteen. After leaving college to get my education by traveling over the United States and Europe, I returned home and took a job my education had prepared me for — the cabbage fields of upstate New York.

At that time, my hair was halfway down my back and about the only outfit I wore was a pair of denim bib overalls and a t-shirt on my 265-pound body. The only job I could hold was in the cabbage fields so that was how I existed — living communally on Lake Ontario in upstate New York.

On the night I received Jesus, I prayed, "If You are real, I invite You into my heart and I will give You two weeks to prove Yourself to me." I was not being sarcastic; I just felt I needed to know for sure before I made such a drastic change in my lifestyle. Within two weeks, I was so certain of the reality of Christ that I could not imagine having missed it all those years.

Shortly after I was born-again, I read Philippians 1:6 in the Bible… "He who began a good work in you will continue until the Day of Jesus Christ." It seemed like there was so much to be done in my life — not only outwardly, but inwardly as well — that it would take forever. But God is God! Overnight, many changes began happening to me.

The people who prayed with me when I accepted Jesus had laid hands on me and prayed, "Oh, God — deliver her from her desire for drugs. Give her Your desires to live within her." I hardly remember the things they spoke, but overnight I was delivered from drugs. The desire was simply gone. It was a miracle!

It seemed to me that it was going to be just as simple to get my weight off. I just knew that if God would deliver me from drugs, He could just as miraculously deliver me from being obesely overweight.

Several days after I was born-again, I was invited to live in a home with single Christian girls. They were all new Christians that went to the same church.

Reluctantly, I moved in with them. I had mostly been in communal arrangements where guys and girls lived together. At the time, I felt that most girls were petty and narrow-minded, but I moved into the house anyway, because I knew that was what God wanted.

Mark 11:23, 24 "...whoever says to this mountain, Be lifted up and thrown into the sea! And does not doubt at all in his heart, but believes that what he says will take place, it will be done for him..." At the time, I weighed 265 pounds, and my roommate was a girl who weighed 240 pounds. As newborn Believers, we just took the scriptures literally and according to Mark 11:23-24, we laid hands on our stomachs and spoke to the "mountain" of flesh saying, "Be thou removed and cast into the sea! — in the Name of Jesus." What would our girlfriends say the next morning when they saw us come downstairs with all that weight off? We were so excited!

Well, it was not quite that easy! But it was a miracle of God because seven months later, I had lost 120 pounds! Believe me; I am just like many of you. I had eaten eggs and grapefruit for weeks at a time. I had tried any diet around and taken every form of diet pill available. I had done everything "in the world" to lose weight but had not succeeded. It was truly a miracle to lose 120 pounds, and I knew God was showing me the greatness of His power.

It all started when one day I read in Proverbs 11:1 that, "Diverse weights are an abomination unto the Lord…" Well, I had no idea that scripture was talking about justice being done on the earth. All I knew was that 2 Timothy 3:16 spoke to me as I read, "[the Word of God] is given by inspiration of God and is profitable for reproof…correction…and for training in righteousness." It chastised me like a sword, and I thought, "I am an abomination unto God!"

"Diverse weights" exactly described me! I was always losing thirty pounds and gaining fifty pounds! I was up and down, so I set about to lose weight and God did a miracle.

During the next four years, many things were changing in my life, and outwardly the difference was apparent. A friend cut my hair into a long shag. I had bought my first dress and was being transformed outwardly into a lady. Life was very exciting, but on the inside, a lot of things were not changing. I felt like a failure. I felt that nothing I could do was right. It seemed that every time I did anything, I just blew it. I was losing any confidence I had, and my body was reacting to the pressure by being sick. It was almost as if I had laid down on purpose. I would tell a friend I had a little headache, and as soon as I did, I found a big headache coming on. The next thing I knew, I was in bed with someone bringing chicken soup and a get-well card. That was happening to me because I did not know my rights or privileges as a Believer. I just let these things come upon me.

Poverty had set in too. I thought it was hard, living from hand-to-mouth in the drug world to make enough money to get drugs for the day. Now as a Christian, I was working every day, but the devil was stealing from me through doctor bills, flat tires, and every possible avenue that he could. I had the best job I would ever have, and yet, it seemed that I could not meet the rent.

At that time in my life, I had lost the majority of my weight, but it was a constant battle. I was a "binger," and whenever I was alone in the house, I would eat everything in the refrigerator. Then I would starve myself for the next ten days so I could tell people the miracle God had done in me. I would panic when my girlfriends came over and asked me to share how I was losing weight and I had just secretly consumed a chocolate cake. I had lost weight, but I did not have victory over my flesh.

The circumstances of life were weighing me down. I did not want to leave God, but I had just decided that I did not want to live in a community of people that seemed to me to be so free when I was so bound on the inside. Have you ever felt that way? As if everybody around you was doing fine, but you were just missing it? That is where I was, and I knew there were some people around me who were feeling the same way.

On the other hand, many beautiful experiences had begun to happen in my life. I was the secretary of my church community. I was the one that was always looked to for counseling, and yet — I was just giving my opinion. It was not even working in my life. The Word of God says in Hosea 4:6, "My people are destroyed for lack of knowledge." Well, that was exactly what was happening to me. I was a born-again Believer, but I was perishing because I had no knowledge of the Word of God. I had no idea what God had already done for me according to His Word.

2

I Cried – He Heard

My heart began to cry out to the Lord, and do you know what happens when you cry out to the Lord? "He hears you in your distress, and He answers you." (Psalm 120:1) That is exactly what happened to me. I cried unto the Lord and said, "God is this all there is? If this is what it is, I might just as well go off and live by myself. I am not going to leave You, but I am just not going to keep up a front with all these other people around me. I am just going off to be alone."

As I cried out to God in my distress, He answered me in a dream. It is the only time I have ever had a dream that had such a dramatic impact on me. In my dream, I was tied in ropes and all these people around me were pulling the ropes so tight that I awoke with cramps in my body. In my dream the only two words I heard were "lies" and "deceit." I was so paranoid that immediately, I thought God was "dealing" with me, telling me I was a liar and that I was deceived. So, I just closed myself off from hearing Him. Within two or three days, God finally got through to me with His message — I was just listening to the lies of the devil, and I was being deceived into not believing His Word.

During the next few months (that was in 1976) the Word of God started coming alive to me. As I cried out to God, He began to unfold His Word to me in a way that I had never seen before.

I had felt like such a failure, but God began to show me in His Word exactly who I was. According to I Corinthians 1:30 and 2 Corinthians 5:17-21, I was the righteousness of God in Christ Jesus.

According to Philippians 4:13 "I could do all things through Christ who strengthened me and infused me with inner strength." "I was born of God's divine sperm." (I Peter 1:23) and "I had the nature" (1 Peter 1:3-4) and "ability of God residing within me to create, and whatever I set my hands to would prosper." (Psalm 1:3)

As He started leading me through His Word, the Word was jumping out and coming alive to me. Hebrews 4:12 says "...The Word of God is alive and active and full of power and is operative and effectual, penetrating down to the deepest parts of the joints and marrow of your bones and it will sift and analyze the very thoughts, intents, and purposes of your heart."

Well, that is what God's Word was doing in me. It was sifting my thoughts and making me realize that what I had thought was not really truth. If I believed in God, then I must believe His Word. For when you make Jesus the Lord of your life, you have to make the Word the Lord of your life. Jesus and His Word are one. So, if Jesus is first place, the Word must be first place.

As God led me through His Word, He talked to me about poverty. Through Philippians 4:19, He said, "My God shall liberally supply and fill to the full your every need according to His riches in glory by Christ Jesus." Then I saw in Psalm 23:1 that because "The Lord is my Shepherd; I should not lack or want for any good or beneficial thing." I thought, "That sure doesn't look like me!"

As I continued on through the Word, I saw more. I saw in Isaiah 53: 1-6 that "Jesus, Himself, had borne my sin, sickness and disease upon the cross that I might die to sin and live unto righteousness, for by the stripes of Jesus I was healed." I saw that "the very same Spirit that raised Christ from the dead, according to Romans 8:11, would quicken my short-lived, mortal body and restore it to health." I got so excited that those things were in the Word! I had just never seen them like this before — the lights were coming on!

I had heard that sickness was a way of God teaching you things. So, when I got sick, I always prayed and asked God to teach me something. He always did, because it was the only time, I ever asked Him. He would always teach me something from it, but it was not His will that I be sick. Jesus had already paid the price for healing and sent the Holy Spirit to teach us through God's Word.

As time went on, God began to show me spiritual tools. I wondered how to get from what I was seeing in myself — what I felt like, looked like and seemed like — to what I saw in God's Word. Since it seemed like I could not get the victory over excess weight, how could I get what Paul said in the Word to be life in me? In Acts 24:16 Paul said ". . . I always exercise and discipline myself [mortifying the deeds of my body deadening my carnal affections, bodily appetites, and worldly desires, endeavoring in all respects] to have a clear (unshaken, blameless) conscience, void of offense toward God and toward men." I thought, "How long will it be before I can say that about myself?" And then the Lord said to me, "You just simply do that. Say it — about *yourself*."

3

The Word — Confession

Now, there was not a word in my vocabulary called "confession" at that time. I did not know what confession meant. I only knew that God was saying to me, "Begin to say about yourself what My Word says about you. Begin to believe what My Word says more than you believe what you feel like, what you look like and what it seems like. Act as if you already are what My Word says and talk about it as if you were."

So when people would ask me if I had enough money to pay the rent, I began to say that "My needs were liberally supplied and filled to the full according to God's riches in glory by Christ Jesus and that I did not have any lack or want of any good or beneficial thing" (Philippians 4:19) so I knew my rent would be paid on time. If they asked what I was going to do tomorrow, I would say, "Well, I have the mind of Christ and do hold the thoughts, intents and purposes of His heart so I know I will do the will of God." And even though there are "many plans in my own mind, He'll direct my steps and make them sure." (1 Corinthians 2:16, Proverbs 19:21; Proverbs 16:9.)

Through confession, I was becoming confident, because what happened to me was not a game — not just parroting promises. What happened was that faith was coming into my ears as I was hearing God's Word out of my own mouth. Faith was growing on the inside of me, and I was seeing my needs met, and that is when God began showing me about the power of the imagination.

4

Imagination Can Be A Tool of God

I had not thought about the imagination as something God could use, but He was presenting it to me as a tool. He reminded me of the vivid imagination I had as a little girl. I lived out in the country of upstate New York and one of my favorite things to do was to go to auctions. That was a place where my imagination really worked for me. I would save my allowance, and when allowed as a child to cross the country roads, off I would go to the auctions. They were held down the road at the Cobblestone Church or Cobblestone Schoolhouse, where everybody would gather with their antiques and junk to sell.

With my two or three dollars, I had to get everything I wanted, so I looked it all over to see what I would bid on. When something was put up for bid that nobody would bid on (like an old mirror that was warped and you could not see in it) they would say, "Give it to that little girl on the front row." By the end of the day my father would often have to come with a pick-up to take home all of my three dollars' worth of belongings.

One day, I bought an old wedding gown, and I was so proud of it. I would get any little boy in the neighborhood to go over to the old Cobblestone Church and practice with me for the day when I would be married. As I practiced, I imagined myself as a beautiful bride being married in a country church. Well, you know, sometimes I thought that would never come to pass, but at the age of twenty-seven, in a little country church on the edge of Fort Worth, Texas, I was married to my husband. It was even more beautiful than I had even imagined.

Another treasure I used to buy at those auctions was old, oak, cane-bottom chairs with the seats broken out. They were beautiful oak under the green paint, but nobody wanted the old things. I would bid ten cents apiece and they would give me the whole lot. So, upstairs of the old barn on our property, I made a lovely playhouse. My dolls were sitting in the broken-out chairs; my cracked china was set for tea parties. Those were beautiful things in my lovely home. Well, now I have my own home. Those same old chairs are in my dining room — refinished and re-caned — and part of my lovely home because I imagined it when I was just a little girl.

One of my wildest imaginations as a child was of being a preacher. My father worked a swing shift so my family did not always go to church, but my grandmother and I would often attend with a little old lady across the street who owned a 1936 Plymouth automobile. I loved to ride in that old car with the little window shade in the back seat. It was so much fun that I would go to church just to ride in that old '36 Plymouth.

During the service, I would take notes and when I got home, I would tell my dad that I wanted to have church. So, my family would all gather together, and my father would make both my brothers sit and listen to me. I knew just four hymns on the piano: *The Old Rugged Cross*, *Blest Be the Tie That Binds*, *Trust and Obey*, and *Blessed Assurance*. I always played the piano and opened with a song and a prayer. Then I would preach a sermon that would always entail how my brothers should treat me. I would close with a benediction and play a closing song. That would be my church service. That is how my family often went to church. Well, look at me today! In my imagination, I saw myself ministering God's Word and now I am.

God brought to my remembrance these things I used to imagine as a child and then said to me, "In the same way you had imagination as a child to see those things that were not as though they were. It is a tool that you can begin to use with My Word."

Even though it does not look like you are exercising and disciplining yourself, see yourself as a victor and act as if you are. Even though it does not look like you are well, get up and by faith say you are, believe it and act as if you are.

5

Praying God's Word

The third thing that God began to impress upon me was that the same Word I was simply walking around confessing, "I am . . . I am . . . I am" could be used in prayer. He showed me that His Word sent forth would not return void but would accomplish what I would send it forth to do. "So shall My word be that goes forth out of my mouth; it shall not return to Me void [without producing any effect, useless] but it shall accomplish that which I please and purpose, and it shall prosper in the thing for which I sent it." (Isaiah 55:11)

One day as I read Ephesians 5:1 telling us to ". . . be imitators of God [copy Him and follow His example] as well-beloved children [imitate their father]." I thought, "Imitate God do what?"

About that time the Lord sent a special gift in the package of a lady preacher named, Billie Adams. She came to the area near my home to hold meetings and to share about praying God's Word. As she spoke of God sending His Word forth to heal and deliver from the pit of destruction, I knew that was one way I could "imitate" God — I needed to send His Word forth in prayer.

Now God's Word became something I not only confessed as mine, but I began to pray it as well that God might watch over His Word to perform it. My prayer life took on excitement as I saw the results of this new tool, I was using to build my life in prayer. Proverbs 14:1 says, "[A] wise woman builds her house, but the foolish one tears it down with her own hands." She will build or tear it down with her own mouth, too! Proverbs 18:20 says, "A man's moral self shall be filled with the fruit of his mouth and with the consequence of his words he must be satisfied (whether for good or evil.)"

Well, up until this time, I was not satisfied with good, but I *was* filled with the fruit of my own lips for evil. Everything that had come out of my lips was negative — "Poor me," "I cannot," "I will never," — and I was being snared by the words of my mouth. But now as the building began, the changing began.

In Proverbs 24:3 the Word of God says, "Through skillful and Godly wisdom is a house, [a life, a home and a family] built and by understanding it is established [on a sound and good foundation]." So, I sought the Lord for what wisdom really was. How do you build a house on wisdom?

6

Nuggets

The Word of God is your very best dictionary. Find your explanation of the Word *in* the Word. There is no better way. In Colossians 1:9-10 and Proverbs 3:13, it says that wisdom is comprehensive insight drawn forth from the Word of God and life's own experiences of victory. I had gained a lot of wisdom, although most of it had come through tribulations and trials. It was the wisdom that says, "Oh, I will know enough not to get in that place again," but I did not know that you could draw actual wisdom from God's Word; that there were "nuggets" — treasures of wisdom hidden — for me in the pages of the Bible.

In finding those "nuggets" — the promises of God — I began to see that I was the righteousness of God in Christ Jesus, even though I did not look like it or feel like it. I believed it because the Word said it in I Corinthians 1:30 and 2 Corinthians 5:21. Then, when I found a scripture in Job 22:30 that said, you can intercede on behalf of those who are not innocent and God will deliver them by the cleanness of your hands, I said, "That is me. I am a clean woman. I am the righteousness of God in Christ Jesus — not because I am goody-goody, but because the Word says so. I can pray and intercede on behalf of people who are not even innocent, and they will be delivered because of the cleanness of my hands."

I began to believe for success and prosperity. In Isaiah 48:17, God said, "I am the Lord your God who teaches you to profit Who leads you by the way that you should go" He was saying to me, "I will teach you how to profit and even lead you in the way that you should go to prosper." According to Psalm 1:3, I learned that everything I set my hand to should prosper and come to full maturity. So, I began to establish my heart on that.

I had just left the church where I had been working so now, I had no job. How was God going to lead me to prosper and come to full maturity? There were two things I set my hand to do: putting up wallpaper and making feather jewelry. As far as I am concerned, the feather jewelry was an original idea from God. I had imagined in my mind one day that feathers would be pretty in jewelry. I carried the thought around for a while and one day, driving down a country road in upstate New York, I saw a hunter proudly displaying a pheasant to a friend. As I drove by, I immediately swung my car around and went back to ask him what he was going to do with the pheasant feathers.

"I have an idea for making pheasant feather jewelry," I said. "Could I have your feathers?"

He said, "Lady, you can have the whole thing," and just handed me the bird!

I went home with my first pheasant to make feather jewelry. Little by little, God began to give me designs and the next thing I knew it was Christmas season, and I was making very good money by selling pheasant feather jewelry. It was exciting because I had set my hand to do it and it was prospering.

7

Exercise and Discipline

With my weight problem, I began to say what Paul said about himself, that he exercised and disciplined himself. I began to speak according to 1 Corinthians 9:27, that ". . . [like a boxer] I buffet my body [handle it roughly, discipline it by hardships] and subdue it, for fear that after proclaiming to others the Gospel and things pertaining to it, I myself should become unfit [not stand the test, be unapproved and rejected as a counterfeit." I prayed that "even though I would find pleasures that are sweet like honey that I eat only what is sufficient for me." (Proverbs 25:16)

The Word of God will apply to every situation of life, and as I began to speak that Word about myself, I will tell you how profitable it was. Whenever a friend would stop in with a fresh baked apple pie, we were delighted. My first reaction would be, "Sure, I will have a piece," but then the Word would rise up within me — just like God's Word says it will do. When God's Word lives in you, "...it will lead you; when you sleep, it will keep you, and when you awaken, it shall talk with you." (Proverbs 6:22) That Word would rise up within me and say, "But, Barbara, you always exercise and discipline yourself and mortify the deeds of your body." The Word was profitable to chastise me and correct me. Then I would say, "Just forget the pie, and give me a cup of coffee."

Pretty soon my body was under subjection to my spirit. I was an overcomer and I had victory. I no longer just lived for today and starved tomorrow. It was victory that came through Jesus Christ, making me more than a conqueror. "Yet amid all these things we are more than conquerors and gain a surpassing victory through Him Who loved us." (Romans 8:37)

At the same time, my health was improving. I was beginning to apply the promises of God and I was walking in health. It was not that I never had an opportunity to be sick or never had symptoms come against me, but when the symptoms would come I would say, "[I] dwell in the secret place of the Most High, stable and fixed under the shadow of the Almighty [Whose power no foe can withstand]." (Psalm 91:1) I would speak to the power of Satan in the name of Jesus and command every symptom of disease to leave my body because Jesus is ". . . the name that is above every name, [and] … at the name of Jesus every name [of sickness or disease] must bow …" (Philippians 2:9, 10)

8

Brazil, By Way of Texas

Still unmarried at age twenty-six, I had decided there must be something wrong with me — nobody wanted me. I even had guys around when I weighed 265 pounds, but now that I was down to 145 pounds, it seemed that every guy I knew was marrying one of my best friends. I thought, "God, there is just nobody here for me." I had roomed with fifteen different girls by that time and had been a bridesmaid for each one. I was really getting depressed and wondered when it would be my turn. I had cried, boohooed, and squalled.

Finally, as I was hearing the Word and getting set free at the same time, I discovered an exciting promise in God's Word. I was on my way from New York to Brazil, by way of Texas. But remember, "Many plans are in a man's mind . . ." (Proverbs 19:21) "*but the Lord direct[s] my steps and make[s] them sure.*" (Proverbs 16:9) I thought God would have me go to Brazil and give myself to working with children in an orphanage for a time. Being twenty-six years of age and single, I felt very noble about the entire thing. I was more noble than intelligent when I left New York and thought Brazil was right below Texas. After all, is not South America below North America? I just planned to drop my car off at Billie Adam's home and fly on to Brazil. I did not realize that it was equal distance from either Texas or New York to Brazil, but I had made my plans and believed the Lord would direct my steps and make them sure. I planned to stop in Tulsa on the way and visit Rhema Bible Institute.

When I arrived at Rhema Bible Institute, I really started making some decisions. Kenneth Copeland was ministering that week and he had been a favorite of mine on tapes. I had become a Kenneth Copeland fan and by that time, I even talked like a Southerner, because I had listened to so many of his tapes.

That week, the Lord started speaking to my heart, instructing me that I was going to stay in Texas. That was an unfathomable thing for a girl from upstate New York, because my only picture of Texas was cowboys and Indians. I wondered what I would ever do in Texas?! But I proclaimed myself to be obedient to God's will.

Before I left Oklahoma, however, I wrote a covenant with the Lord in my prayer book, and it is precious to me even today. The covenant I wrote was that He would be with me exactly as His Word said He would be. I also wrote that He was going to go before me to prepare a way, prepare my work and prepare my living place. I put Him in remembrance of

His Word. Now, I know He had not forgotten it, but I needed to hear it.

I had decided that I was going to be obedient to God's will and go to Texas, and now I wanted a mate. I was tired of being double minded about it. I did not want to be alone anymore. I wanted to know what God's Word said about it. I already knew that "He who finds a wife finds a good thing and obtains favor of the Lord" (Proverbs 18:22) and I was just waiting to be found! (You have to believe you are a good thing if you want a man to believe it!) I was building my life on God's Word, expecting myself to be a blessing to a man, but I did not know how to pray God's Word for a mate.

At that time, I came across a scripture promise in Isaiah 34:16. (All you single women will be interested in this one.) "…none shall want her mate [in fulfillment]; for the mouth of the Lord has commanded, and His Spirit has gathered them." I thought, "Praise the Lord! My search is over! "The Spirit of God will go forth and gather my mate and thrust him into my path." I began to say it, I began to pray it, and I began to believe in my heart for the husband that was not, as if he were.

I began to pray for my husband as if I already knew him. I prayed according to Philippians 1:27, that ". . . we would stand firm in united spirit, striving side by side and contending with one mind and one purpose for the Gospel's sake." I prayed according to Romans 15:5-7, "that we would live in mutual harmony and full sympathy with one another; that we would always with one voice and one heart, praise and glorify the Father of our Lord Jesus Christ." Before I even knew who my husband would be, I believed according to Proverbs 2:16 that "...discretion watched over [my husband] and kept him

[away] from alien women and from the outsider with her flattering words." I was building in prayer then for the harmony we enjoy in our home now.

I prayed according to Proverbs 5:15 that we would "... drink waters out of [our] own cistern [of pure marriage relationship], and fresh running waters out of [our] own well."

I prayed according to Proverbs 5:17 that when we had children, "they would be for us alone and not strangers in our own household." I prayed my husband would be absolutely, "... always transported with delight in my love" and "my ...bosom would satisfy [him] at all times," according to Proverbs 5:19. Well, that is what the Word of God said, and I believed it!

9

God Prepared My Husband

So, I arrived in Texas with the Word of God going forth to prepare my husband. My friend, Billie Adams, took me to my first Vicki Jamison Crusade and it was a delightful evening. Vicki and Billie were very close friends and Vicki invited us to a banquet after the service.

When I walked into the auditorium and took my seat that night, the Lord spoke to me and said, "That man down there is the man that I have thrust into your path to be your husband." I was pretty excited and pondered ways I could let this man know. Instead, I said, "Lord, Your Word says that You watch over Your Word to perform it...and that is exactly what I am going to let You do. You simply watch over Your Word to perform it." (Jeremiah 1:12)

That evening at the banquet, I was introduced to Stephen Arbo (God's man), and we had an instant rapport — it was amazing. We were the only two young people there, and we just talked and laughed together the whole evening.

The week I arrived in Texas, a friend of Billie's was visiting from California, who was a make-up consultant. She had taken one look at me and said, "We ought to get a little make-up on you and get those eyebrows plucked." So, between Billie, Martha McGee, and Peg Nichols (my friend visiting who was a hairdresser) they transformed me to the point that even I hardly knew myself.

When I was introduced to Stephen that night as Barbara Wells, who had just arrived from New York, he thought I must have been a model from New York City. So, he felt he surely could not have anything to do with me. And there I was thinking, "Boy, what a 'country bumpkin' I am. That guy probably does not want anything to do with me." Four long months passed without hearing from him. However, during that time, God was doing a work because, you see, I had learned the power of praying God's Word and found out exactly what it could do.

The thing that concerned me most about this man I met, who was someday going to be my husband, was that he weighed about 285 pounds. He was a handsome, tall Canadian, and very attractive to me. But I thought to myself, "God, if You would do it for me, I know You would do it for him. If I send Your Word forth on Stephen's behalf, You will deliver him from that pit of destruction."

So, I went home that night and said to Billie, "I think I am going to get to know that fellow a little bit better." (I did not want to say, "I know I am going to marry him!") Instead, I said, "I am going to begin to pray the Word of God for Stephen to lose weight." So, I sent God's Word forth in prayer.

Now, an alternative would have been to simply go to Stephen that night and say, "Stephen, I used to weigh 265 pounds and I have lost a lot of weight through the power of God's Word. You just take it, pray it, and be obedient to God's Word. It can change your life. When you get your weight off, come see me, because God has told me I am going to marry you." I do not think I would have ever seen him again.

I continued to pray for Stephen that summer and would see him once a month at crusade meetings, but he never seemed to pay much attention to me until he was literally thrust into my path in August of 1978.

Finally, taking a giant step to go out on my own in the big city of Dallas, I went to a concert at the Bronco Bowl. The auditorium seated about 3,500 people, which is more than the population of my hometown. I took a seat and began visiting with the people next to me, thinking how bold I was to come by myself to the big city for a night. As the lights dimmed, I was surprised and thrilled to see somebody I knew, Stephen. He walked by me, and we exchanged greetings then he went on his way hunting for a seat.

Suddenly, two people sitting by me decided to move and the lady next to me said to Stephen, "Here is a seat. Here is a seat." So, Stephen was, literally, thrust into my path that night at the Bronco Bowl. He asked for my telephone number that evening and six weeks later, we were engaged to be married!

I turned to him that night with great excitement. "Stephen, you are looking so good. What has happened to you?"

He replied, "I do not know, the weight is just falling right off me."

He had lost 75 pounds. I really got hold of the power of God's Word in prayer at that point. I thought, "This is just something else! How God does work!"

Now, I know we all pray beautiful prayers, and I encourage you to keep praying the way you always pray, but when you start to find out how God watches over His Word, you will want to learn how to pray God's Word, too. You see, Jeremiah 1:12 says, "He hastens to watch over His Word to perform it" — not ours.

10

My Parents Shall Rejoice

About the time I came to Texas, I became concerned about my family's attitude toward me. My parents were disturbed about the life I had been living and our relationship was pretty much broken. First, I had been on drugs, then I became a Christian and was living in a little Jesus community, then I had taken off for Texas. They just did not know what to think and I could not blame them. They were glad I was not doing drugs anymore, but they were concerned about me and certainly did not rejoice over all that I did.

I looked for a scripture and knew that if I could find a promise in God's Word, it was mine. I found a scripture. It was Proverbs 23:24-25, which said, "The mother and the father of the uncompromisingly righteous child shall be glad and rejoice in that child. The father who becomes the father of a wise child shall have joy in him and the mother who bore that child will rejoice and be glad." I thought, "That is for me!"

I began to send God's Word forth in prayer that my mother and father would rejoice over their uncompromisingly righteous child that I had now become. I believed I was a wise child because I was now drawing forth wisdom from the Word of God and from my life's experiences of victory. I began to send the Word of God forth that it might not return void.

As I sent it forth, about three weeks later, I received a letter from my mother saying, "Barbara, we are so happy for what you are doing. We are pleased at what is happening in your life. We are so glad you are our daughter. We are so proud of you!" The Word was coming back exactly the way I had sent it forth. It was just like a mirror reflecting right back on me the image I had sent forth.

11

My Interim Period

Now there was a period of time between my learning the principle of speaking the Word and when I could actually speak it forth as I do now. I call it "my interim period." It was when I did not have a thing to say. I had learned to stop talking about all the negative things. I had learned not to talk about my problems. Mark 11:24 says, "When you pray believe [at that point] that you receive them...." And so by faith, I did not have any problems. I did not know anything good to say yet. I did not want to talk about the bad. I just simply did not have a thing to say. My friends did not like it. They were all saying the same thing.

"I do not know what is wrong with Barb. She has just changed. She is different. We used to enjoy her being around, but now she is always listening to tapes or reading the Word.

I do not know what the matter is with her." And these were my Christian friends. I am not talking about unbelievers. I am talking about Christian brothers and sisters.

The devil was immediately trying to steal the Word from me, which is the same thing he will try to do after you read this book. Because when the Word of God gets planted, Satan comes immediately to steal the Word. It is the Word he wants, but he will come with circumstances. He will come as if to destroy your marriage. He will come as if he wants to put your children on drugs. He will come as if he wants to keep you from having enough money to pay your car payment this month. He will come as if he wants to keep you from losing those ten pounds you so desperately want to lose. What he really wants is simply the Word! He wants to convince you that God's Word is not alive and full of power, and it will not work for you. That is what the devil was doing with me at that time, but I stayed with the Word, and it gave me victory.

You see, the Word of God says in Ephesians 6:13, "Having done all to stand, [you] stand some more." People ask me, "Well, how long do you pray and stand on God's Word?"

My answer is always the same — "Having done all to stand, simply stand some more, because the Word of God will never return void. It will always accomplish the purpose that you send it forth to do."

What happens within you is that you will get an established heart. Psalm 112 talks about the man who has an established heart. It says that man will not be moved forever — the man whose heart is established on God's Word.

12

Confession: It Is For You

Some people think confession is a game — you say it and God does it, but you see, confession is not for God — it is for you. Every time you speak forth the Word of God, faith comes to your ears by hearing it. The picture is painted on the inside of you. You see that thing, you believe you have received it, and it has become substance within you. That is the Word becoming flesh and dwelling in you.

In the beginning, it was just a word that there would come one named, Jesus, and that He would be the Savior of all mankind. God had spoken it, but it was just words. That is all there was to it. "There shall be one born unto a virgin, Mary." They were just words, but then "…the Word became flesh and dwelt among us." (John 1:14)

In the beginning, it may be just words that you exercise and discipline yourself, mortifying the deeds of your body and deadening your carnal appetites and bodily desires. In the beginning, it might be just words that you and your husband walk ". . . side by side with one another in harmony, striving with one mind and one purpose for the Gospel's sake." (Philippians 1:27)

In the beginning, it might be just words that "All your children are disciples — taught of the Lord [and obedient to His will]; and [have] great . . . peace and undisturbed composure." (Isaiah 54:13) They might be just words when you begin, but as the Word becomes substance on the inside of you, then the Word becomes flesh, manifesting itself in answered prayer.

One of the first things that will begin happening in your life as the Word of God dwells within you richly — more abundantly than any other source or thought — is your telephone calls will probably begin. That is what happens when the Word of God lives in you, because you have Life to give. After my little interim period of having nobody talk to me, pretty soon my telephone rang off the wall. People would call saying, "Barbara, I have this problem and I just do not know what to do about it." I would say, "Well, let us just pray and agree according to God's Word."

I started out with the most valuable tool that I ever had, and that was a little prayer notebook. In it, I made different headings on subjects concerning me. What concerned me when I first began hearing the Word was the salvation of some of the people that I loved dearly. So, I put a tab in for salvation so that I would know what God's Word said in 2 Timothy 2:26, that those people were going to ". . . come to their senses and escape out of the snare of the devil . . ." and serve God forevermore.

From 2 Corinthians 4:4, I understood they were blinded [by Satan] and prevented from seeing the illuminating light of the Gospel. That helped me to see that they did not simply *not* want to listen to me — they were not opposed to hearing about Jesus — they were blinded. So, I could pray according to Ephesians 1:17-18, that ". . . the eyes of [their] heart be flooded with light so that [they could] know and understand what is the hope to which He has called [them] and how rich is His glorious inheritance in the saints — His set-apart ones."

I put a tab in my prayer notebook for weight because that was a problem that concerned me at the time. I put one in for employment because I did not have a job, and I needed a reminder that I was worthy of my hire and that God could lay a door wide open before me that no man could shut.

Whatever the situation was, I put it in my prayer notebook, because God was going to perfect those things which concerned me. That is what Psalm 138:8 says. When you cannot remember another scripture and you are in some circumstance of life, you say, "Oh, God, I wish I knew a Word." Pull out Psalm 138:8 and say, "God, all I know is You perfect those things which concern me today and watch over Your Word to perform it." This gives you confidence, because God is saying, "If you will ask anything according to My will, you will know that I will hear you." 1 John 5:14 says that this is how you can be certain that He will hear you . . . because you ask according to His will. His Word is His will. If you know that He hears, you can certainly know that you will have the petitions that you have asked for.

13

Praying In Confidence

Praying God's Word is a way of praying in confidence so that the devil cannot come in and say, "That is impossible, it cannot happen, God just cannot do it." You refer back to the Word and say, "It is written, devil. It is written."

For those who are battling with an overweight condition, it is written in 2 Timothy 1:7, that ". . . God did not give us a spirit of fear but [He has given us a spirit of] power and of love, of a sound mind, discipline and self-control." Is that revelation to you, too? I did not know I had been given a spirit of self-control. I was looking all over for it. When I found out I had been given a spirit of self-control then I could speak to the devil and say, "It is written." He had to flee the same way that he did when Jesus spoke to him in the wilderness. Matthew 4:10 "Be gone, Satan: for it is written . . ."

Now, the most important thing to remember about praying God's Word is simply this: God is the One who watches over His Word to see that it comes to pass. God says in Jeremiah 1:12, "I hasten to watch over my word to perform it." You do not have to make God's Word work.

Isaiah 61:11 explains it like this — ". . . as surely as a garden will cause what is sown in it to spring forth, so surely shall the Lord cause rightness and justice and praise to spring forth before all the nations through the self-fulfilling power of His Word." Through its self-fulfilling power!

"The Word of God is alive and active and full of power… [It is] operative… [It is] effectual..." (Hebrews 4:12) The Word will work for itself. You are simply a co-laborer, a fellow workman with God, planting the Word by speaking it forth, backed by faith. For "faith is the substance of things [that you] hoped for…" (Hebrews 11:1) Things that are just dreams, imaginations and hopes — to you. Proverbs 13:12 says "Hope deferred makes the heart sick, but when desire is fulfilled, it is a tree of life." God wants to fulfill your dreams and desires.

14

Speaking God's Word

The most important way you can pray God's Word is by praying according to 1 Timothy 2:1-2. "First of all, let prayers and supplications be made on behalf of all men …and those who are in positions of authority…" If there ever was a day for us to pray for those in authority it is today. As we pray for those in authority, we will live peaceable lives. If you want a peaceable life, start praying for those who are in authority. Start sending God's Word forth that discretion watches over them and keeps them from the way of evil men and women, from the outsiders who are alien to God. Pray that skillful and godly wisdom will enter into their hearts and lead them and guide them, and their hearts will be in God's hand like a water brook. Proverbs 21:1 tells us that when, "The king's heart is in God's hand as are the watercourses; He turns it whichever way He will." (Proverbs 16:3) Well, this is true for kings, presidents and all those who are in authority. You see, He can even cause their thoughts to become agreeable with His will so that God's plans will be established and have good success.

The added benefit of praying God's Word is that it gets down on the inside of your spirit and the Holy Spirit can bring it forth anytime. I have not memorized scripture. The Word of God that comes out of me has been planted in there by speaking God's Word to others and by praying God's Word. I just discovered one day that it was on the inside of me.

I would talk to somebody about the problems they were having in their marriage, and I would say, "Well, let us just believe that you will let all the bitterness, wrath, animosity, bad tempers, evil speaking, slanders, and abusive language be banished from you and your husband. I pray you will begin to live in harmony and love with one another, being tenderhearted toward one another and forgive one another readily as God in Christ Jesus has forgiven you." (Ephesians 4:31-32)

I had prayed that for people who were having disharmony in their homes and all of a sudden, I realized it was on the inside of me. It just rose up exactly like the Word says it will do. It will rise up and speak with you and when you lie down it will keep you.

Isaiah 50:4 was the very first scripture that I ever prayed, and it makes this prayer. "Father, in the name of Jesus, I am a disciple taught of the Lord, and you have given me the tongue of those who are taught. You awaken me morning after morning." (I was a late sleeper but was trying not to be one. Then I found this scripture that said the Lord awakens me morning after morning — now I am a 6:00 a.m. person.) I confessed, "The Lord awakens me morning by morning to hear as a disciple. I do not turn my back (roll over in bed!), neither am I disobedient, but I hear the Word of the Lord and I always know how to speak a word to the weary one in due season." And that became my goal — to have a word for the weary one in due season and quit giving them my opinion.

If you have ever had people coming to you, saying, "I just do not know what I should do in this situation. What do you think I should do?"

You know it is an awkward place to be because some people will actually take what you think and do it, and that can be dangerous! I would much rather have them do what the Holy Spirit wants done.

When friends began to call with their questions, I would say, "Well, I will tell you what — I think you ought to move to Dallas. Lots of things are happening here and we could have lots of good times. I just think if you have an opportunity to move your business here, you ought to do it. I think it is a good idea." And they would say, "Oh, I do not know, We have been thinking about it but just do not know what we ought to do. God has us here, but if we just thought that was what God wanted."

Then they would not go around saying, "Barbara thinks we ought to move to Dallas!" They would just say "Barbara believes that the will of God will be done in our lives, and I do too, because faith has come to my ears by hearing God's Word, and I believe that I do the will of God. I believe that I hear the voice of the Lord and another voice I do not follow. I am a disciple taught of the Lord, obedient to God's will."

My friends and I were just like most of you. At one point I had so many different decisions to choose from — plan A, B, C and D. I thought I would like to work with Vicki Jamison-Peterson. Also, I thought I could minister in Germany and move to New England. I wanted to live out in the country and raise a family. There were all kinds of things I would have liked to do! But I chose to follow God's plan. Because the Holy Spirit leads and guides me, I am assured in my heart that I will do the will of God and be obedient to God's will, for I am a disciple taught of the Lord. I am obedient to God's will, and I have great peace and an undisturbed composure. (These were all dreams I had in 1981 when this book was first published, and I've done all of them!)

Today, rather than confusing people more with my opinions, I pray and agree with them that according to God's Word in 1 Corinthians 2:16, "[You] have the mind of Christ and do hold the thoughts, feelings and purposes of His heart." And according to Proverbs 21:1, "Your heart is in God's hand like a water brook, and He can turn it withersoever way that He would. Your path is shining more and more, brighter, and clearer until the day of Jesus Christ and even though there are many plans in a man's mind (Proverbs 19:21) the Lord directs his steps and makes them sure. Even though it seems as if the lot is cast into your lap, the decisions you make will be wholly of the Lord, for even those things that right now appear to be a circumstance are just simply steps that are ordered by God." (Proverbs 16:9 and Proverbs 16:33)

This goes for you, too. When you speak the Word of God over your life you will do the will of God. You will end up doing exactly that, because God watches over His Word to perform it on your behalf.

15

God's Word Within Rises To Speak

The Word gets on the inside of you. It rises up to speak; and the Word on your lips is a wellspring of life — living water to those around you. Proverbs says that once you have found a way of life yourself, you are a way of life for other people. (Proverbs 10:17) It is great to get all the situations in your own life ironed out. It is great for God to perfect those things which concern you, but somehow in my heart, I feel like God leads us this way and shows us how to get the concerns of our own lives perfected so that we'll realize that the same power is available to get the plans and purposes of God moving for His kingdom. We can use these same principles to lay doors wide open for ministry and for other situations that God wants to perform on the earth — in your neighbor's life, in your friend's life, in your family's life. You can begin to take authority and send God's Word forth on their behalf.

Years ago, I got a call from upstate New York, from my mom saying my father was on his deathbed with cancer. I had just been in Texas for a short time and, of course, my immediate reaction was much like yours would have been. I wanted to run home and be with my daddy. At that time, my father was not born again. Ever since I had become a Christian, when I would talk to my dad about Jesus, he had jokingly said this to me, "Oh, Barbara, that is great for young people, but what is the sense of doing all that now? I can receive Jesus on my deathbed. The way I smoke these cigarettes, I will probably be there with cancer someday anyway." Somewhere he had been told that, and that is what he believed.

Proverbs 18:20 says "A man's moral self shall be filled with the fruit of his own mouth ..." and my dad was now on his deathbed with cancer. It was not great that he was on his deathbed, and it was not great that he had cancer, but it was great that he had said he would get saved on his deathbed. That is exactly what happened. I had asked some friends to go minister to him and my father was born again in the hospital.

I wanted to go home, but at this point, God had assured me that I could simply send His Word forth and not have to go myself. So, I began to send God's Word forth in prayer, declaring that Jesus Himself had borne my dad's sin, sickness, and disease upon the cross; that he now, being dead to sin, would live unto righteousness and by the stripes of Jesus he was healed. (Isaiah 53:4-5; Romans 6:11; 1 Peter 2:24)

Within a couple of weeks, we were getting good reports and my father's surgery went beautifully. They had removed all the cancer and were expecting him to do very well. We were all rejoicing through our prayer circles in Fort Worth at what God was doing in my dad's life. God was perfecting that thing which concerned me and now my dad was born again, which was even a greater reward.

One night about two weeks later, the Lord spoke to me. Some of you are wondering how God speaks to people — if He just walks around talking to them — but never does to you. I will tell you how God spoke to me that night. I was playing a Vicki Jamison album and as she sang these words, the Lord was speaking to me, "Freely, freely, you have received. Freely, freely give. Go in My name and because you believe, others will know that I live." That is how the Lord spoke to me to go home and minister to my family, and that because I believed others would know that He lived.

The next day I thought, "Lord, two weeks ago everybody wanted to pay for my plane ticket home and was encouraging me to go. Now, I have told them I was not going, and I do not have a cent. How am I going to get there?" But I knew God told me to go and by the following morning, He had provided everything I needed.

That afternoon, I got on an airplane and arrived home just in time to greet my whole family. They were gathered together as I pulled into the driveway.

My mom said, "Barbara, I just knew you would come."

My father was to have emergency surgery and they were on their way to the hospital. A problem had developed, and they were going to remove a portion of the colon and put a colostomy on his body. They did not expect that it would ever be repairable.

My father wanted to die rather than live with that thing. He had just made up his mind, he would be better off dead. He had already been prepared for surgery when I got to the hospital.

I said, "Dad, you will live and not die, and in the name of Jesus, the same Spirit that raised Christ from the dead will quicken and restore to life your short-lived, mortal body and you will not have to have the colostomy."

Well, I know faith came to his ears and he wanted to believe me, but like everyone else who had heard the doctor's report, it did sound pretty wild for me to say something like that. Three hours later, he came out of surgery with a colostomy. "It seemed as if my whole family was looking to me for what to do next. I spoke of those things that were not as though they were.

Things seen are always subject to change. 2 Corinthians 4:18 says "...the things that are [seen] are temporal, [they are] brief and fleeting [they are passing away]. but ..." "The Word of [God is eternal; it will last forever.]" (Isaiah 40:8) (1 Peter 1:24-25)

I was assured of God's Word even though the doctors were saying the colostomy would be permanent. There was hope in God's promise "for the things *seen* are temporal and subject to change."

Two weeks later, when I had come back to Texas, my father called on the telephone and said, "Barbara, I have good news for you. The doctors do not know how it has happened, but the x-rays show that my colon is able to function on its own and they have to take this colostomy off."

You see, because the Word did not return void, it had accomplished the purpose I sent it forth to do. The Lord perfects those things that concern me, and He will do the same for you.

16

He Perfects Those Things . . .

One day while visiting my dad in the hospital, he turned to me and said, "Barbara, you look beautiful."

All the weight was off and so many changes that God was doing outwardly in me, as well as inwardly, were evident.

He said, "Barbara, you look beautiful to me. You know, I just wish your teeth could be straight."

My parents had spent a lot of money for braces on my teeth when I was young, but the orthodontist did not do the job right. Two of my front teeth were still noticeably out of line. I found myself answering, "Dad, I believe they will be."

He asked me if I thought God would do that and I told him, "I am sure He will — either by a miracle or by providing the means for another way. Well, Dad, just pray."

I believe Dad prayed, because when I got off the airplane in Texas, my friend who picked me up at the airport said, "Oh, Barbara, by the way, I went to a party while you were gone and saw an old high school friend who is an orthodontist now in Fort Worth. I was telling him your testimony about what God has done in your life, and he and I have decided to share the expense together, to straighten your teeth as an offering unto the Lord."

At that time, it did not seem really thrilling to have braces and when he told me they would have to be on for three years, my first reaction was to balk. Then I thought, "God, You perfect those things which concern me, and if this is the way You are going to do it, I have got to follow through with this."

So, I began to use my faith and look at those things that were not as though they were. Two days after I had the braces on, Steve proposed. We made plans to be married eight months later.

I started believing God that in eight months, He was going to do the work on my teeth that would normally have been done in three years. I never told the orthodontist what I was believing. He just kept saying, "They are looking good. They are really moving fast."

The Saturday before my wedding day, he removed those braces and gave me a retainer to work with inwardly after that. Praise God! He perfects those things which concern me

— whatever they are — and I do not have to tell you something he did ten years ago. He is still doing things now.

One day I wanted some trees for my yard. Steve and I had bought a house in Dallas and the former owners only planted a couple of trees in the yard. Coming from the country of New York with beautiful foliage everywhere, I just could hardly stand living in a place with no trees.

I was on my way to New York that week and had to leave on Monday morning, but thought, "Oh, Lord, it is time to plant, and I really want to get some trees in our yard." Everywhere I looked, they seemed so expensive, and I could not figure out how to get enough money to plant trees before I left.

That weekend before I left, we visited friends on Saturday morning. As we were leaving, their neighbor was mowing his lawn for the first time of the season.

I just yelled over to him, "Boy, that is a nice sight." He stopped the mower and came over to talk.

He said, "Say, you and your husband could not use some trees for your yard, could you? We have just put a new waterline through our property, and we had to dig up all these trees and I just do not have time to plant them. They have to be planted within forty-eight hours."

Well, that was exactly how much time we had before I was to leave. The man told us that day he would not guarantee the trees would live, but we prayed over them in planting. When he stopped over to see us later, he told us our trees were fuller and in better shape than the ones he left in his yard!

Those kinds of things are what make Jesus real to you. I love to be able to pray with the authority and to send God's Word forth for healing and deliverance, but to have God perfect those things which concern only you — which no one else really even cares about — is just so special. You can watch God's Word at work; alive, active, and full of power on your behalf.

It gives you incentive to do something about the fact that your loved ones are unsaved. You do not have to accept that it is a cross in your life to bear, as you have been told. You can pray that they come to their senses (2 Timothy 2:26) and that the eyes of their heart be flooded with light (Ephesians 1:17, 18) and for the perfect laborer to be thrust in their path. (Matthew 9:37-38) You can begin to have harmony in your home as you send God's Word forth, and it gives you something to do. I guess God's people have always wanted something to do.

Well, if I am going to do anything, it is going to be praying God's Word and letting Him watch over it to perform it. It is just like the day when the angel came to Mary and said, "You shall bear a son." (Luke 1:31) If I had been Mary, I would have said, "Okay, just tell me how it is going to happen and let us get it over with, because I have plans of my own." Mary could not make the Word come to pass. She could not do it. She just said, "Be it done unto me according to Your word." (Luke 1:26-38) And God watched over His word to perform it and brought forth Jesus. He wants to bring forth Jesus in each of our lives.

If you are reading this book and you did not even know anything like this existed — if you do not know Jesus — He is never perfected anything that concerned you, it is because you just do not know him. I want you to receive Him today and begin to let Him work in your life, in all the different situations that are important to you and concern you. Just stop and ask Him to come into your heart and become your Savior, Healer, Deliverer, and Friend.

Some of you reading this have had all kinds of circumstances come against you. Your children are gone, and you do not even know where they are. You think they might be on drugs, but you do not know what the situation is. Know that according to God's Word, "Your children have not been brought forth for sudden terror or calamity, but to be the blessed descendants of God" (Isaiah 65:23) "[For God] will contend with him who contends with you and..." give safety to your children and ease them." (Isaiah 49:25) You can "Restrain your eyes from weeping and your eyes from tears . . . And your children will return from the enemy's land." (Jeremiah 31:16) to be ". . . disciples — taught of the Lord, and obedient to God's will; and great will be the peace and undisturbed composure of your [children.]" (Isaiah 54:13) If you will begin to see that thing that is not as though it were "*they may come to their senses and escape from the snare of the devil.*" (2 Timothy 2:26) henceforth to serve God forevermore.

In the following pages, I am going to share with you a portion of my own prayer notebook. I have chosen subjects that I trust will help you in your own life and in ministering to others. These are not all the scriptures in the Bible on any given subject, but I trust they will give you a start in learning to pray God's Word.

If you begin to pray these scriptures, you will find that rather than having memorized them, they all will make their home in your heart, rising up to speak with you; and when you lie down, they will keep you. Your words will be as choice silver and you will be a vessel of honor, ready for the Master's good use, pouring forth the living Word, which is life to all who attend to it, and healing and health to their flesh.

> Job 22:25 "And make the Almighty your gold and the Lord your precious silver treasure."
>
> Proverbs 25:11 "A word fitly spoken and in due season is like apples of gold in settings of silver."
>
> 2 Timothy 2:21 "So whoever cleanses himself [from what is ignoble and unclean, who separates himself from contact with contaminating and corrupting influences] will [then himself] be a vessel set apart and useful for honourable and noble purposes, consecrated and profitable to the Master fit and ready for any good work."
>
> Proverbs 4:20-22 "My son, attend to my words, consent and submit to my sayings. Let them not depart from your sight keep them in the center of your heart. For they are life to those who find them, healing and health to all their flesh."

Prayer Scriptures

First of all, let us get it settled in your hearts and minds that it is God's will for your friends and loved ones to be saved. Luke 19:10 says, "...the Son of man came to seek and to save that which was lost." That is the reason the Son of God came — so it is certainly His will to see that accomplished! Next, understand that the unbelievers you are concerned about are blinded, according to 2 Corinthians 4:4 which says, "...the god of this world has blinded the unbelievers' minds (that they should not discern the truth), preventing them from seeing the illuminating light of the Gospel of the glory of Christ, the Messiah, Who is the image and likeness of God." It is not that they do not want to hear you talk about Jesus, they just cannot "see." You have been given authority to bind the powers of darkness, and now you can pray that their eyes are flooded with light.

Salvation

Ephesians 1:17-18

[For I always pray] the God of our Lord Jesus Christ, the Father of Glory, that He may grant you a spirit of wisdom and revelation — of insight into mysteries and secrets — in the [deep and intimate] knowledge of Him, By having the eyes of your heart flooded with light so that you can know and understand the hope to which He has called you and how rich is His glorious inheritance in the saints — His set-apart ones.

Matthew 9:37-38

...The harvest is indeed plentiful, but the laborers are few. Therefore, [I] pray the Lord of the harvest to force out and thrust laborers into His harvest and (bring them across _____________'s path)

2 Timothy 2:26

...that they may come to their senses and escape out of the snare of the devil — having been held captive by him, henceforth to do God's will.

Remember, as you pray for others . . .

Job 22:30

He will deliver the one [for whom you intercede] who is not innocent; yes, he will be delivered through the cleanness of your hands.

What makes your hands clean? What makes you a righteous man? Jesus has been made unto you righteousness (1 Corinthians 1:30 and 2 Corinthians 5:21)

Will of God

Every one of us needs to be secure that we are walking in God's will at every moment of every day. As you pray these scriptures, they will establish your heart on the fact that God's will is being accomplished for you at all times. You will walk about confident that the decisions you are making are right, and that your mind is the mind of Christ, following His intents and purposes.

Ephesians 5:17

[I] will not be vague and thoughtless and foolish, but rather understand and firmly grasp what the will of the Lord is.

1 Corinthians 2:16

...[I] have the mind of Christ ... and do hold the thoughts (feelings and purposes) of His heart.

Colossians 1:9-13

[I pray and believe this day that I am] filled with the full (deep and clear) knowledge of God's will in all spiritual wisdom [that is, in comprehensive insight into the ways and purposes of God] and in understanding and discernment of spiritual things; that [I might] walk (live and conduct myself) in a manner worthy of the Lord, fully pleasing to Him and desiring to please Him in all things, bearing fruit in every good work and steadily growing and increasing in (and by) the knowledge of God — with fuller, deeper and clearer insight, acquaintance and recognition. [I pray that I might] be invigorated and strengthened with all power, according to the might of His glory [and] to exercise every kind of endurance and patience (perseverance and forbearance) with joy.

Ephesians 1:17-19

[For I always pray] the God of our Lord Jesus Christ, the Father of Glory, that He may grant [me] a spirit of wisdom and revelation — of insight into mysteries and secrets — in the [deep and intimate] knowledge of Him, by having the eyes of [my] heart flooded with light, so that [I] can know and understand the hope to which He has called [me] and how rich is His glorious inheritance in the saints — His set-apart ones, and [so that [I] can know and understand] what is the immeasurable and unlimited and surpassing greatness of His power in and for us who believe, as demonstrated in the working of His mighty strength.

Ephesians 4:23-24

[I am being] constantly renewed in the spirit of [my] mind, having a fresh mental and spiritual attitude; and put[ting] on the new nature...created in God's image (Godlike) in true righteousness and holiness.

Ephesians 5:15-16

[I] look carefully...how [I] walk! [I] live purposefully and worthily and accurately, not as the unwise and witless, but as the wise — sensible and intelligent...making the most of [my] time...

As you can see, sometimes I simply spoke God's Word forth as my confession of faith. Once I pray myself or others into the scriptures, I follow up my praying by confessing that I believe it to be true, according to God's Word.

Weight

Since I was having a battle with excess weight when I made my prayer notebook, this was a "large" section. Some scriptures were my prayer of faith, others were to help build an image on the inside of me of an overcomer and several to use as swords against Satan, saying, "It is written, it is written, it is written." Among these scriptures, you will find several that will be profitable for any kind of habit.

1 Corinthians 6:12

Everything is lawful and permissible to me, but not all things are helpful and good for me to do. Everything is lawful for me, but I will not become the slave of anything or be brought under its power.

2 Timothy 1:7

For God did not give us a spirit of timidity, of cowardice, of cravings, but He has given us a spirit of power, and of love, and of a calm and well-balanced mind, DISCIPLINE and SELF-CONTROL.

I Corinthians 10:13

For there is no temptation — no trial regarded as enticing to sin that has overtaken [me] that is not common to man. That is, no trial or temptation has come to me that is not adjusted and adapted and belonging to human experience and such as man can bear. But God is faithful to His Word and to His compassionate nature and can be trusted not to let [me] be tempted and tried and assayed beyond my ability and strength of resistance and power to endure, but with the temptation He will always provide the means of escape to a landing place — that I may be capable and strong and powerful to bear up under it patiently. Therefore, I will shun, keep clear from, and avoid by flight if need be, any sort of loving anything more than God." (This sent me out of the house running more than once!)

Proverbs 25:16

When I find pleasures sweet like honey, I pray, I will eat only what is sufficient for me, lest being filled with it, I vomit it up.

Proverbs 23:1-3

I pray I will consider what is before me when I sit down to eat and put a [spiritual] knife to my throat, if I be given to desire. I pray that I not be desirous of dainties, for they are deceitful food offered with questionable motives.

Acts 24:16

Therefore, I pray and believe that I will always exercise and discipline myself — mortifying my body (deadening my carnal affections, bodily appetites and worldly desires) endeavoring in all respects to have a clear, unshaken, and blameless conscience void of offense toward God and toward man.

I Corinthians 9:27

Like a boxer, I buffet my body, handle it roughly, discipline it by hardships and subdue it, for fear that after proclaiming to others the Gospel and things pertaining to it, I myself should become unfit — not stand the test and be unapproved and rejected as a counterfeit." (Personally, I felt this was a battle I must overcome to free myself in order to share the power of God with others. I had to know it could work in my own life.)

Romans 8:37

Amid all things, I am more than a conqueror, and gain a surpassing victory through Him who loves me.

2 Corinthians 4:18

...for the things seen are temporal, fleeting, and passing away, but the Word of God is eternal. *(I claimed this for the excess weight I "saw" telling my body it was subject to change!)*

Harmony in Marriage

If you allow God to watch over these words to perform them, submission will be no problem to you, and you will live in harmony and peace with one another.

Romans 15: 5-7

May the God who gives the power of patient endurance (steadfastness) and who supplies encouragement, grant _______ and I to live in such harmony and such sympathy with one another, in accord with Christ Jesus, that together we may with united hearts and one voice praise and glorify the God and Father of our Lord Jesus Christ — and that we will welcome and receive to our hearts one another, even as Christ welcomed and received us for the glory of God.

Romans 13:13

Let us live and conduct ourselves honorably and becomingly as in the open light of day, not in reveling, carousing and drunkenness, not in immorality and debauchery (sensuality and licentiousness) not in quarreling and jealousy.

Proverbs 5:15-19

Father, I pray and believe that _________ and I will drink waters out of our own cistern of pure marriage relationship and fresh running waters out of our own well. That he/she will confine himself/herself to me alone and our children will be for us alone, and not the children of strangers with us–that our fountain of human life will be blessed with the rewards of fidelity and that we will rejoice with each other. (Wife) — I pray that I will be as a loving hind, tender, gentle, and attractive, and my bosom shall satisfy ____________ at all times and he will always be transported with delight in my love.

Colossians 2:2

I pray that _______________ and my heart may be braced, comforted, cheered and encouraged as we are knit together in love, that we may come to have all the abounding wealth and blessings of assured conviction of understanding, and that we may become progressively more intimately acquainted with and may know more definitely and accurately and thoroughly that mystic secret of God which is Christ, the anointed one.

Ephesians 5:33

I pray and believe that_______________ will love me, his wife, as being in a sense his very own self, and that I (wife) do respect and reverence my husband — that I notice him, regard him, honor him, prefer him, venerate and esteem him, that I will defer to him, praise him, love and admire him exceedingly!

Philippians 1:27

I pray that ________________________ and I may stand firm in united spirit and purpose striving side by side and contending with a single mind for the faith of the glad tidings (the Gospel)

1 Corinthians 13:4-8

I pray and believe, Father, that our love will endure long, and be patient and kind. Our love will never be envious or boil over with jealousy. It will not be vainglorious and will not display itself haughtily. May our love not be conceited, arrogant, or inflated with pride; not rude or unmannerly and not act unbecomingly. God's love is in us and I pray we will not be self-seeking, touchy or fretful and resentful, taking no account or paying attention to a suffered wrong. I pray we would not rejoice at injustice but rejoice when truth and right prevail. May our love bear up under anything and everything that comes and be ever ready to believe the best of each other having hopes that are fadeless and enduring without weakening. Because love never fails, I pray God's love in us will never fade out or come to an end.

Healing

Psalm 103: 2-3

I bless you, Lord, with all my soul, and forget not all Your benefits — You heal all manner of diseases. Father, Jesus Himself has borne my sin, sickness, and disease in His own body that I might be dead to sin and live unto righteousness, and by His stripes I was healed. The chastisement needful to obtain my peace and well-being — spirit, soul, and body — was paid for on the cross and I thank You for healing me. (Also see Isaiah 53: 3-5; 1 Peter 2:24)

God's Word tells us in Psalm 107:20, that God sent His Word forth to heal and deliver from a pit of destruction. That same Word sent forth in prayer is still healing and delivering. As you learn to walk in the divine health Jesus purchased for you, be a vessel to send God's Word forth on behalf of those who are not innocent that they might be delivered by the cleanness of your hands — the righteousness you have from Jesus Christ. (Job 22:30)

Romans 8:11

Father, I pray that the same spirit that raised Christ from the dead will quicken and restore to life this short-lived, mortal body.

Hebrews 4:12

I pray that the Word of God [which] is alive and active, and full of power will penetrate down to the deepest part of the joints and the marrow of bones.

Proverbs 4:22

...for your Word is life to all those who attend to it and healing and health to all of their flesh.

Luke 10:19

Father, Your Word says we have been granted physical and mental ability over all the power that the enemy possesses. I take that authority now and command every symptom of sickness and disease that is named to bow to the name of Jesus — the name above every name, to which every other name must bow.

Here are some references for specific health concerns:

- Amputation — Proverbs 3:26
- Arthritis - Hebrews 4:12
- Blind, Deaf — Isaiah 29:18
- Broken bones (preventative) — Psalm 34:20
- Eyesight — Isaiah 32:3
- Heart - Psalm 73:26

- Speech Impediment - Isaiah 32:4
- Stomach trouble — Exodus 23:25
- Weakness, Fainting - Isaiah 40:29

Prosperity

Psalm 112:1-3

Lord, I thank You that I am a blessed man (woman) because I fear the Lord, and delight greatly in Your commandments. Wealth and riches shall be in my house.

Philippians 4:19

...for my God liberally supplies and fills to the full my every need according to His riches in glory by Christ Jesus.

Psalm 23:1

...And because the Lord is my shepherd, I will not lack or want for any good thing.

Luke 6:38

Father, I pray that as I give, it shall be given unto me, good measure pressed down and shaken together and running over, men shall give unto my bosom.

2 Corinthians 9:6-9

As I give bountifully, I pray I will reap beautifully, for You, Lord, are able to make all grace abound toward me that always I may have sufficiency to meet my own needs, and an abundance to give to every good work and charitable donation.

Proverbs 10:4

Father, thank You for accomplishing Your Word in me, causing me to be a diligent man (woman), made rich.

Isaiah 48:17

Lead me in the way I will profit, Lord, and teach me to prosper.

Psalm 1:1

I believe Your Word, Father, that I am a blessed man (woman), walking in Your counsel, and everything I set my hand to do, I pray, will prosper and come to full maturity.

Proverbs 3:9-10

As I honor You, Lord, with my capital and sufficiency from righteous labors, and with the first fruits of my income, I pray You will fill my storage places with plenty.

Psalm 34:10

The young lions may lack and suffer hunger; but I pray that as I seek You, Lord, by right of my need and on the authority of Your Word, I will not lack any beneficial thing.

3 John 2

I know because it is Your will above all things that I prosper and be in health even as my soul prospers, You will bring it to pass in my life.

John 10:10

…for the thief comes but to steal, kill, and destroy, but You have come that I might have life and have it more abundantly. I receive an abundant, prosperous life in Jesus' name!

Joshua 1:8

As I keep Your book of the law in my mouth, meditating on it day and night, I pray I will make my way prosperous and deal wisely in all my affairs in life, having good success.

Your Home

A home can be such a special place of refuge, surrounding you with peace and precious things. Proverbs 24:3 tells us that by skillful and godly wisdom a house, a life, a home, and a family built, and then by good understanding it is established on a sound and good foundation. Verse 4 goes on to say that by knowledge shall its every chamber be filled with pleasant and precious riches. Is anyone believing for some new furniture? God wants you to have the desires of your heart, (Psalm 37:4) remembering always that the most precious treasure in your home is His presence — for there we find fullness of joy (Psalm 16:11)

Psalm 107:7

I pray that You might lead us forth by the straight and right way, to a city where we might establish our home.

Proverbs 3:33

Thank You for blessing the habitation of the just — those in right standing with You.

Proverbs 12:7

Because our home is that of the righteous, it will stand, even when the wicked around us are overthrown.

Psalm 91: 1, 10

As we dwell in the shelter of the Most High God, I pray that no evil befall us or any plague or calamity come near our dwelling place.

Psalm 122:7

I pray that peace will reign within the walls of my home, and prosperity with it.

Salvation Prayer

"The Word of God is alive and full of power…" Hebrews 4:12. Your confidence in God and His ability to watch over His Word and perform it in your life comes from a personal relationship with Christ. As you grow to know Him, you will experience for yourself His promise to perfect what concerns you. The first step comes as you open your heart and acknowledge your faith in God.

Why don't you pray right now and ask Him into your heart? Pray this simple prayer:

> "Lord Jesus, I believe You are the Son of God. I need You in my life. I want to know You for myself. I want to experience Your love and understand Your Word. I open my heart to You now and receive You as my Lord and Savior. Help me to grow in the understanding of all that you did for me when you went to the cross. Thank you for a new beginning for my life. Now I am born again!"

NOTES

Please visit our website arbominstries.org
for more information on how to purchase other books
and audio messages.

If you would like to have Steve and Barbara minister
in your area, please contact our office
at 1-800-276-2726.

Additional contact information:

Arbo Ministries
14 Curtis Road
Gilford, New Hampshire 03249
arboministries@gmail.com

You can also follow our ministry on Facebook
at New England Sanctuary or on
YouTube @barbarastevearbo.

www.ingramcontent.com/pod-product-compliance
Ingram Content Group UK Ltd.
Pitfield, Milton Keynes, MK11 3LW, UK
UKHW062256290726
14090UKWH00017B/726